kl♡pp
actually

(Imaginary) Life with Football's
Most Sensible Heartthrob

Laura Lexx

First published in Great Britain in 2020 by Two Roads
An Imprint of John Murray Press
An Hachette UK company

1

Copyright © Laura Lexx 2020

The right of Laura Lexx to be identified as the Author of
the Work has been asserted by her in accordance with
the Copyright, Designs and Patents Act 1988.

A CIP catalogue record for this title is
available from the British Library

Hardback ISBN 978 1 529 34821 7
eBook ISBN 978 1 529 34822 4
Audio Digital Download ISBN 978 1 529 34823 1

Typeset in Miller Text by Hewer Text UK Ltd, Edinburgh
Printed and bound in Great Britain by Clays Ltd, Elcograf S.p.A.

John Murray policy is to use papers that are natural, renewable
and recyclable products and made from wood grown in sustainable
forests. The logging and manufacturing processes are expected to
conform to the environmental regulations of the country of origin.

Two Roads
Carmelite House
50 Victoria Embankment
London EC4Y 0DZ

www.tworoadsbooks.com

For Moose, who I love in real life

Contents

Why on earth does this book exist?

This is a weird idea for a book right? An imaginary diary of being married to a person I know next to nothing about? I'm going to set the scene, because this book is bizarrely context-sensitive considering it bears almost no literal connection to the circumstances from which it was born. I need to take you back to 13 March 2020 when I was holed up in an ibis hotel in Glasgow thoroughly petrified of the incoming pandemic and trying to take my mind off Covid-19.

I idly tweeted a silly joke about this football manager I'd noticed a few weeks back . . .

If I ever met Jürgen Klopp I'd say 'omg if we have a baby we should call it Klipp' just so he'd raise an eyebrow at me and tell me I'm a moron and I'd be so naked by the time he'd finished doing that.

That was it. Why Jürgen Klopp? Well, because I'd seen him get asked a question about the pandemic-shaped horizon and he'd had this to say . . .

Look, what I don't like in life is that for a very serious thing, a football manager's opinion is important. I don't understand it. I really don't understand it . . . It's not important what famous people say. No, we have to be able to speak about things in the right manner, not people with no knowledge, like me, talking about something. People with knowledge should talk about it and should tell the people, 'do this, do that, do this and everything will be fine, or not.' Not football managers, I don't understand that.

I mean . . . WHAT?! Who does that? Who says 'sorry, I'm not an expert – ask someone else?' In this day and age?! NO ONE! That's why we have a journalist for a Prime Minister and social media is largely a hell hole of know-it-alls. No one is sticking to what they know . . . except . . . him.

This was the beginning of my absolute crushing admiration for Jürgen Klopp. It seemed to me that this guy was a different breed: a hero for our times. With a bit of digging I discovered he was a football manager, with a bit more digging I found out football is the main game taught to boys at school.

Having wasted twelve years of my life learning how to land on one foot and pivot with the other foot in netball lessons, I don't have much of an attachment to football.

So, why was I in Glasgow? I'd travelled there from Brighton for a weekend of gigs: I'm a stand-up comic – or at least I was before 2020, you remember in the version of the world where you could sit uncomfortably close to people in a dark basement? It was great! I'd drive to a place, make some strangers laugh and then go home.

Hopefully by the time you're reading this (probably an A-Level text or whatever A-Levels are called in 2054 when this is considered a literary master-piece) everything I'm about to describe sounds too mad to be real. Like when people talked about ration books when you were at school and you thought, 'Of course they had ration books and could cope with it; it was the past when life was harder and people didn't mind because they were sturdy.' Well, let me tell you future person: in 2020, when corona hit, we minded.

I'd got the overnight train up thinking I'd crawl into a private cabin and slumber until I woke up in the magical world of Scotland. Instead, I was awake for every second of that journey trying to analyse every cough as if I'd suddenly become a disease specialist. The gigs were lively but tense; we were all pretty sure that by the next weekend pubs and gigs would be closed and so were trying to make the most of this freedom while also not being entirely sure that we were safe doing so. The country was on the precipice of shutting down, but it hadn't happened yet and we all felt really weird. Lockdown would end my entire income and cancel my career. But that was too much to think about, so instead of making a plan, I carried on tweeting . . .

I'm quite stressed out by all this 'real life' stuff going on but one thing really keeping me sane are these hopping mad fantasies about marrying sensible Jürgen Klopp.

We'd go to IKEA and I'd be like 'oh this lamp is so cute' and he'd say 'No Laura we are just getting the things we came here for.' But then at the till he'd let me have a bag of Dimes anyway cos I'm cute. Then we'd drive home in our nice Volvo.

We'd be getting ready to go out on a Saturday and I'd say, 'Do I look fat in this?' and he'd say, 'you have a pretty reasonable body fat amount I think but if you're unhappy here are some fitness regimes you could get into.' And then we'd sensible fuck.

I'd ask him what he wanted to watch on TV and he'd say, 'Actually, I've already had a lot of screen time today I think I will do the vacuuming and then read my book. Unless there's anything you'd like to do?' And then even the pants I wasn't wearing would be ruined.

We'd be snuggled up on the sofa and I'd say 'oh my god babe I saw on Twitter earlier that the govt are going to . . .' & he'd say 'do you have at least 2 corroborating sources?' And I'd say, 'no, but . . .' & he'd say, 'well then don't share it like facts.' And my bra would snap off.

I'd lean over to him and say, 'what's the most craziest thing you've ever done . . .?' And he'd take off his glasses, look me in the eye with THOSE blues and, rubbing my cheek with the back of his hand he'd say . . .

'Once, driving on the motorway, this guy was in the middle lane the whole time not caring how much worse it makes the road for everyone else. So when he pulled over into a service station I killed him with bare hands.' He blinks at me hoping I understand and BAM I'm so pregnant.

Every morning he'd eat Weetabix because it's 'not that sugary crap' and I'd have my pop tarts and he'd roll his eyes but not criticise out loud because he's not been to medical school so it's not his area of expertise.

For Valentine's Day he'd learn all of the characters in the *Gilmore Girls* and the complex forces that drive Lorelai and then he'd set aside 2.5 hours for us to discuss the show. He'd know better than to mention 'those extra ones'.

At Christmas, he'd calmly hold my mum's hand and explain that my lack of appearance on *Mock the Week* is not indicative of my career being a failure. She'd listen and believe him and stop mentioning it for almost 3 days.

We'd be cuddled up in bed and he'd take a really cute selfie of us and even though I looked hot I'd say, 'ah please don't put that on Instagram I look gross' and he'd look at me sternly and say 'I don't have Instagram, I'm a grown man with a job' and then we'd open-mouth kiss.

He'd buy me a box set of DVDs of old episodes of Transworld sport.

I'd offer him a biscuit and he'd say 'No, it's ok, I am not hungry.' And I'd say, 'darling don't be silly you don't eat biscuits because you're hungry, you just eat them until there aren't more.' And he'd tuck my hair behind my ear and say 'I think this is why you are unhappy.'

Walking home from the dry cleaners having collected his baseball caps for the upcoming week, he would take my hand and say 'Your short legs have terrible stride efficiency, I would not play you up front.' And I'd say, 'you played me up front last night' and he'd smirk knowingly.

Unable to find him, I'd peer out the window and see he's in the shed again, angry. I'd take him a cup of tea, 'you ok?' I'd ask. 'Yes,' he'd reply tersely. 'Idiots comparing the BBC licence fee to the cost of Netflix again?' But the pain in his eyes would be all the answer I need.

'What you doing?' I say sidling up behind him.

'Sending emails as you can well see, Laura,' he replies.

'Haha, if you signed off with your initials it would be like – AH I WAS ONLY JOKING THIS WHOLE EMAIL. That'd be funny.'

'Laura if you suggest that once more we will divorce.'

I went to bed after that one. It was about 1 a.m. and I had twitchy eyes from refreshing Twitter and chatting with people who were laughing and interacting. I said I might do some more when I woke up and I went to sleep nervy, but somewhat distracted and amused.

The next morning I was too scared to go outside because I didn't have a mask or hand sanitiser. Again, future scholar of this pivotal moment in time when fan-fiction became as revered as historical drama, you need to get your head round what was going on: masks and hand sanitiser were impossible to get hold of at this point of the pandemic. People had gone ballistic in supermarkets; they bought up all the pasta and toilet roll as if when corona knocked on the door pretending to be the gas man they could knock it out with a well-aimed farfalle. Meanwhile hand sanitiser was being hoarded in lock ups by 'entrepreneurs', or 'bell-ends' as we called them at the time, and the average person couldn't seem to buy a bit of it even if they were willing to sell a kidney.

I spent all of that Saturday hiding from the real world, but unable to tear my eyes away from the internet looking for updates and information and hope. That day it just felt like we were ALL on the internet trying to use it like a periscope to look over the horizon and see when lockdown would get here. To distract myself between terrifying graphs, I jumped back into this fantasy world of a really sensible and fulfilling partnership, and I carried on tweeting.

'Good morning,' he says, rolling over.

'Don't look at me, I look awful without make-up,' I say, pulling the duvet over my face. 'Make-up is a falsity you do not need,' he says shortly, & I lean in to kiss him. 'It's toothpaste you should worry about in the mornings.' And he gets up.

'We are late,' he calls from the hall.

'I don't have any shoes to go with this dress,' I wail, and he enters the bedroom. 'Are you planning any elaborate styles of motion tonight?' he asks.

'No' I sniff, staring at his dappled beard for comfort. 'Well then any shoe will go on your body at the same time as this dress.'

He picks up a shoe and slides it onto my foot, as his hand touches my calf my dress flies off. 'You can't go out that like though,' he smiles sternly and we miss the party to bang with regular water breaks.

'Will you still love me when I'm old?' I ask him, feeling needy and insecure.

'It depends what has happened in the intervening years,' he says looking up from the variety of newspapers he reads.

My knees go weak & we couple well away from the newspapers so they're not spoiled.

His hand slides over my bare back, every nerve in my body knows we will soon be one. 'Tell me I've been a bad girl,' I say, looking up at him through thick eyelashes. '8 times today I have had to turn lights off after you. You are more than a bad girl.' He turns out the ninth light.

He's looking at me so intensely. 'What are you thinking about?' I ask.

'I was wondering whether I love you more than football.'

I blush. 'And what did you decide?'

He takes a slight breath. 'I do not, no. But I love you more than 5 a side.' I am powerless in the wake of his honesty.

It's Tuesday and we've just finished watching an 8-part in-depth true crime doc. 'My god that was intense,' I say, 'Do you think he did it?'

'I do not know,' he says.

'But which way are you leaning?' I ask, lip quivering in excitement.

'I know none of the people involved nor have I seen any of the evidence or had training in this field. It would be irresponsible to make up my mind based on something made for entertainment.' He's in my mouth before the sentence is over.

He is behind me so quietly and quickly that I don't notice. He kisses the top of my head gently and takes the box out of my hand. 'Put that back,' he says softly, 'the supermarket own brand one is just as nice and for half the price.' We hold hands all the way to the frozen aisle.

'I'm going to put a wash on, is there anything you want me to put in?' I call through to the front room.

'Anything I need washing is in the wash basket already as that's where it should be. Yes, I've removed all pocket tissues.'

The humidity in my pants causes a faint whistling.

'I can't persuade Klipp to eat her crusts,' I complain late one night over a glass of red.

'Why should she?'

'Aren't they good for you?'

'It's the same dough as the rest of the loaf just cooked more. It has no greater nutritional value.'

I slide off the sofa for various reasons.

I wrote and imagined until I ran out of steam for that day. It was amazing how many people were having a laugh with me and enjoying this alternative romance. There were only two ways to be on the internet that day: worrying about Covid-19 or dreaming about a relationship like this one. When I started chattering I had about 8,000 followers, but within forty-eight hours I had 40,000. At one point Marian Keyes and Philippa Perry were asking if we could be friends. Emma Kennedy wanted me to write a book. Seth Meyers was waking up America with my writing. Piers Morgan thought I was sexist . . . It was a really good day. My funny little romance world in which a sensible man is sensible was a sensation.

On Sunday 15 March I travelled back down to Brighton, knowing it was the end of live comedy for who knew how long. Certainly at the time of writing, we still don't have an answer. Luckily for me, my little fantasy dream came back home with me as I began to realise quite how much that thread had captured people's hearts. It was humbling and mind-blowing. I was soon in meeting after meeting discussing the potential for a book. It was, quite honestly, incredible; a dream coming true from the ashes of a nightmare. I began the task of turning my short, sweet tweets into a proper thing. This is what I came up with. I hope you like it.

January, February, March

'When I say, "Can you do dinner?"
he understands that part of "doing
dinner" is deciding what to have.

I'd be on the landing in our massive house, making use of the airing cupboard we would definitely have, and that I would fully understand the purpose of . . .

He emerges from the bathroom with the cardboard toilet roll cylinder in his hand.

'Where are you going with that?' I ask.

'To put it in the recycling,' he says. 'I finished the previous roll so I got a new one and have put it on the holder.'

My heart thumps wildly within my rib cage and I am on him before he can take another step. His lips find my ear; his breath hot against my skin.

'I hung it with the loose end over the top rather than against the wall. Just the way you like it,' he whispers, and there's a moaning sound that is not just the cistern refilling.

We'd be indoors on a rainy Sunday, doing the same thing we'd be doing if it was sunny, but feeling less guilty about it . . .

'It's not working,' I say, throwing the controller down in a strop. 'The buttons don't respond when I press them.'

He looks up at my video game avatar bobbing uselessly on the screen. He picks up the controller and tries a few moves himself before inspecting the buttons.

'You might be right,' he concedes gently, 'The buttons might be deciding to misbehave for you but work perfectly well for me . . . or, perhaps you are hungry?'

He leads me into the kitchen, but a sandwich is not the first thing I put inside me.

We'd be at the supermarket buying a healthy balance of proteins and fresh, seasonal, local produce in recyclable packaging . . .

Our daughter, Klipp, is screeching in that pitch unique to toddlers who are actually fine but just not currently the centre of attention. I can see that the woman pushing the trolley next to mine is rehearsing a speech about my parenting skills. It will include her top tip for how to get this child that she has never met to stop crying, and I will have to nod and smile while she delivers it. Worse still, Klipp will probably absolutely adore the top tip and begin to behave herself immediately – but the advice will never work again once the woman is out of sight.

My daughter sits atop her steel cage-carriage begging any passer-by to rescue her from the torment of her captor. Whose heart wouldn't melt at the sight of this literally Pampered Princess and her desperation to be away from the evil witch who will neither let her play with a broccoli nor chew a Toilet Duck while they shop. She is bereft. Channel

4 should make a documentary on the hardships she faces down these murky aisles.

I steer the trolley away, looking for the till with the shortest queue so that we can get home quickly and I can keep her quiet with sugar and a screen like a good mother. I choose the till with the frowning woman scanning tins at a rate of knots. Her speed is mesmeric – dry hands shooting out and gripping the curvaceous tins before sliding them sensuously across the flat glass scanner until it emits its affirmative beep. I have only taken one step towards the queue when a hand appears on the end of the trolley and stops it in its tracks. It only took one arm. I scan the aisles for a handy wet floor sign.

'Let's go to this checkout,' he says, his eyes fixed on a lane at the far end. Back up near the bakery aisle – is he mad? They never put the best people there. I eye the young man behind that till with disdain. His reach is sloppy and his eye wanders across the other people milling about. He lacks focus. I would estimate his till is emitting at least eight blips per minute fewer than the scowling crone at my till.

'No, I think this one will be quicker,' I say, leaning my shoulders into the trolley handles and using my body weight to shift the trolley back. Every muscle in my body is no match for his iron wrist. I barely notice his core twitch as he resists my pressure. It is a fearsome sight. The mutipack bag of Hula Hoops wobbles and so do I. Klipp ceases her griping to see which of her parents will win the battle. The broccoli lies forgotten in her chariot.

'Look at the queues though,' he says patiently, and I follow his line of thought. My till has a very sweet-looking older gentleman waiting to buy a basket load of shopping. His till has a man in a suit, using a mobile phone, waiting with a small trolley of branded items. 'I agree you have chosen the best player – but is she going to have the right game for the opposition?'

He's right, of course, and I feel like a novice. I have already been cornered once in the bakery aisle by that older gentleman, and I discovered more about his colonoscopy than I ever wanted to know. I had to put my doughnuts back.

I shake my head at my amateurish strategising and let my beloved steer our trolley to behind the rude yet efficient suited man who will have nothing to say to the young checkout assistant. As I load

Hoegaarden and Bratwurst onto the moving coun-
ter, I watch from a distance as the old gentleman
pokes a finger in and out of a hoop made from his
other fingers. I can taste caramel cream in the back
of my throat, and I turn away in disgust.

I glance admiringly at my husband; he always
sees the entire pitch, even when most people would
be distracted by the star player. Every item I place
on the juddering conveyor belt feels intense and
exciting. Suddenly it's me who wants to play with
the broccoli.

*We'd go for walks in the evening as
though purposeless wandering was
better than TV . . .*

He closes the front door behind him. We're in the
hall and the tension is electric. I can barely move. I
can only stare at him across the polished wooden

floor. He steps in close, I smell the soap on his skin. His hands find the zip on my jacket and pull it down; confident, strong.

'You should take this off,' he whispers into my ear, 'or you won't feel the benefit outside later.'

If we were walking through the park and a football came our way he'd be so quick and accurate passing it back and all the lads playing football would be like, 'Woah, did you see that?' And I'd be all smiley like 'heh heh heh that's my husband' and then we'd carry on with our day . . .

'Have you got the fifteen?' the woman in the corner shop asks him. She's a sour old biddy who eyes me and Klipp suspiciously, as though we are wearing matching family ankle tags.

'I do not, my apologies,' he says, considering the coins on his palm and then smiling briskly at her.

'It's just, I've not got many 5ps left,' she says, inspecting the contents of the till drawer, and then looking back at him expectantly.

I feel a cold sweat trickle down my spine. If this were me, I would have already mumbled to her to keep the change just so we could be out of the shop before she started scowling and muttering about how often I buy wine. Klipp is trembling by my side, I can see in her eyes she's not sure if her Skittles are worth this. My husband is made of sterner stuff though and he straightens.

'Are you saving them for another customer?' he asks, his voice staying just on the right side of polite. She is flabbergasted. No one talks back to her – she is the keeper of the Doritos.

'No . . .' She stumbles, and he puts one past her defences in a perfect nutmeg.

'Then I will have one of the few you do have and we will both be happy,' he says.

At pubs and restaurants we'd be that table everyone was envious of: laughing loads but not in an annoying way. He'd be a well big tipper too . . .

We're out for drinks with old friends, catching up, exchanging long stories and sharing plenty of laughter. He stands. 'What would you like to drink, everyone? It's my round.'

I glance at my empty glass – gosh, is that another wine gone already? I'd barely noticed. I've inherited the family talent for not noticing I'm shitfaced until I'm starting an argument over something I couldn't even bring myself to start to care about when sober. I make a mental note to warn Klipp of this gene. It's disturbing me how many new things I realise I need to warn her of every day. Her teenage years will not be fun.

My thoughts are interrupted by the sound of my husband gently clearing his throat. He raises an eyebrow at me, expectant of my order.

'Oh, I probably shouldn't have another one,' I finally say, already envisaging the white wine headache that

29

will be curled at the foot of my bed waiting for me in the morning. A hangover I can handle, but when it's multiplied by a toddler it's like being on *The Crystal Maze* after recently getting run over.

'Don't be boring!' crows my old school friend, which instantly makes me feel frumpy and old. 'We barely get to see you as it is – don't go all "Poor me, I've got kids now, I couldn't possibly!"'

All the good spirit suddenly drains out of my evening and I shrink into my chair. The white wine goblin has sanded down the fortress round my self-esteem. It crouches in my brain, sniggering at how easily my friend's words have stung me. I don't feel sad about not having another drink – I waited years to have a tiny me who wanted to play DUPLO at 6 a.m. Perhaps I am a bad friend though; is this what my friends think of me since I had Klipp? This would be a difficult thought to chew on even without 500ml of Chenin Blanc eroding my defensive walls. I try to think of a jokey way to brush it off, but Richard O'Brien is screaming 'thirty seconds' and both my legs are in plaster.

I lock eyes with my husband, smile, and say, 'Oh go on then – one more can't hurt.' I try my best for bright and bubbly. I am a good friend despite the squatting goblin scooping out handfuls of my innards and pelting them onto the floor. I receive a curt nod from my darling as he sends an unseen scowl at the back of the head of our friend.

He returns a few minutes later, his masterful fingers grappling four glasses at once – holding them tight against each other. Not a drop is spilled. From the glasses.

I take a sip of my wine and am surprised to feel cool water with a splash of lemon cordial slip down my throat. He smiles and winks at me from across the table. I am both grateful and hydrated in equal measure. Hydrateful.

I find that, despite my best intentions to be a good friend, I am still utterly distracted from the conversation by thoughts of how I will say thank you later. With his one careful stroke he has dominated my penalty area. When we get home, I find his concern for my fluid intake is, mercifully, unabated.

I'd do a proper weekly shop instead of waiting until I was hungry and then buying whatever the nearest shop sold . . .

I enter the kitchen to find him using up the last of the old butter before starting the new one. My heart races. He eases off the plastic lid with expert fingers and then gently peels back the entire foil. The soft, creamy, pale yellow surface is exposed; forced to wait expectantly for his knife, while he takes the foil covering straight to the bin. I might faint. I feel light-headed and floaty as he takes his first bite of buttery toast, teeth breaking into the bread and chewing silently.

Then, without warning, he releases the catch on the crumb tray under the toaster and empties it without a word. I slide down the front of the cabinets, coming to a halt on the floor, still gazing at the scene. He hears me and turns, looking concerned to see me so ashen-faced and floppy on the floor.

'Would you like a bite of my toast?' he says. When I come to, I have the strangest sensation that it was all a dream, but the taste of butter on my tongue tells me it wasn't.

He'd get home from work and I'd be all nodding and listening and saying 'Ugh, sounds like you were totally in the right' when he had difficult stuff going on . . .

A handsome shadow falls across my desk. I look up from the sentence I am wrestling into place. It's supposed to be a joke, but it's currently a weak observation spliced with a tedious political opinion. The sort of line that onstage would elicit agreement not laughter. It's a modern joke.

The owner of this dapper shadow is a welcome distraction from both the joke, and the fear that I am wasting my life wrestling jokes instead of doing something helpful.

'Laura, I am sorry to disturb you,' he begins, his words delivered precisely as though it is taking a huge amount of energy to remain calm. 'I am unable to find the remote control. It is not here in this remote control caddy that we purchased and that I have mentioned to you several times.'

I close my laptop. The joke is now the least of my worries. It is cold in this majestic shadow. There is more to this than a missing remote control.

Despite my husband's profession, I have still not really managed to wrap a passion for football into my heart. I tolerate it as one does the weather: it changes in pitch, frequency, temperature and the stress level it induces, but it is mainly discussed on television by dull men in front of a green screen.

I rarely attend matches for fear of distracting my husband, or of finding out that I do not distract my husband. (I know which one my fragile ego would find harder to bear.)

They speak of 'the football season', but as far as I am aware the football season takes an entire calendar year to go full cycle. I believe there might be a day somewhere in early July, every other year, where football is not happening. On that day there is twenty-four hours of programming in which the men in front of the green screens discuss how much they can't wait to have football back.

The working life of my beloved is to be gauged as one might a menstrual cycle. I can tell how close we are to some sort of final or important situation by how much not being able to find the remote control annoys him. If he swears at the remote control then it is an important game. If he accuses the remote control of hiding, then it is a very important game. If he comes to find me holding the caddy for the remote to ask why on earth I, a grown woman of reasonable intelligence, am not capable of returning the remote control to the very item whose sole purpose on this earth is to cradle the remote control . . . well, then I know it is a final.

The remote control has been the pawn ever since we got soft-close cupboards. Before the days of soft-close cupboards I had a kitchen-based alarm system like a troupe of howler monkeys but now the jungle is quiet.

I follow him down to the living room and help him look for the missing buttons. We discover I have left them beside the plant pot that I had finally remembered to water because I had just switched over to *Springwatch*. Curse you Packham and your persuasive ways.

The unfinished joke upstairs in my laptop can wait; right now my husband needs me and so I brew us each a cup of tea and ask him if there's anything I can do to help.

It turns out he is furious with a colleague of his that I don't think I have met. It may be one of the assistant coaches or something, but from what I can gather he must have got his job through nepotism because no one seems to think he's very good at it. It has been one bad decision after another.

As my beloved's tirade comes to an end I smile and shake my head sagely, 'There's nothing for it my love, you are simply going to have to fire this Var guy.'

My advice clearly settles his mind because he simply smiles, picks up the newly recovered remote control, and switches on the television without another word.

We'd both be working from home on stylish laptops at the dining room table . . .

'I'm hungry,' I say, knowing full well I am just bored.

'Are you?' He raises an eyebrow at me sternly. 'You want to put something in your mouth, do you?'

'Yes,' I reply, giggling. 'I'm desperate for it.'

'Have some fruit,' he says, and returns to his laptop.

I'd be all like, 'yeah, I work eighty hours a week – I just live to work, you know?' And people would nod as if that wasn't the saddest thing they'd ever heard . . .

As I drag my weary bones up the stairs to bed, I recoil at the sudden memory of stripping the bedding off before I left for work.

'Bollocks,' I think to myself, knowing I won't be able to fall straight into an exhausted sleep. A fight awaits me behind the bedroom door: a boisterous tussle with an ethereal, weightless ghost. I have lost weeks of my life to the inside of my duvet cover. Nothing fills me with a greater frustrated fear than this task. When the oxygen starts running low, and you're scared you'll never find your way out, half expecting to discover David Bowie's Goblin King round every cotton corner. How have we managed to get jet planes to carry three hundred people across an ocean, but we've not solved how to peacefully encourage an enormous downy naan bread into a sedentary cloth envelope?

When I push open the door to the bedroom, though, he is stood under a beam of light like an angel, or Mr Bean. The bed is fully made. He's even noticed that the buttons go at the bottom of the bed.

'You've put fresh sheets on?!' I exclaim, loving him more now than that time he pretended he didn't think Margot Robbie was particularly attractive.

'Of course,' he says, bemused by my joy. 'I have never understood why you don't do the whole job at once. There is no sense to leaving half a job for when you are most tired. If you win the game in the first half, you only need to defend in the second.'

My tiredness dissipates as I watch him Febreze his cap and climb into bed. By morning we no longer have a clean sheet.

I'd have a conventional body size and shape and could just order things online knowing they'd turn up and look normal on me . . .

'I have nothing to wear,' I wail, staring despairingly into the wardrobe.

'This is a lie, you have lots to wear, you just don't believe you look good in it,' he replies. I am about to argue with him, but I haven't got an answer to his pinpoint accuracy. 'So if you think you look bad in everything, it really doesn't matter what you put on.'

I may believe I look bad in things, but I know what I look good on.

I'd be looking all cute in my fluffy dressing gown while we enjoyed some time on the sofa together . . .

He is tensed on the edge of his seat, peering keenly at the screen. His back is curved as he crouches over the remote control. He is poised like a tightly coiled spring waiting for the exact moment he needs to hit pause.

His attention to detail for how best to stroke the buttons is something I have always admired in him.

That which in reality played out over only ninety minutes has become a four-hour replay marathon, as he repeatedly pauses to analyse and consider before restarting the tape. He is methodical, thorough, allowing no glance or movement to go unnoticed as he scours the action for moments he missed.

He reaches the end of the tape and sits back contentedly on the sofa.

'Shall I make us a cup of tea before we go through these notes?' he says, indicating the notepad. I nod. It is not exactly how I had envisaged us watching our wedding video back, but this is undoubtedly the man I married.

We'd be out for dinner, somewhere real posh with cloth napkins . . .

He looks at me across the table. He is more than handsome. Apollo in a polo shirt. The flickering light from the candle reflects in his glasses. He has already told me off twice for playing with the wax – I never could resist playing with fire.

'Would you like a dessert?' I say, lowering my menu.

He eyes me carefully, as though daring me to gather that tantalising pool of molten goo into a squashy, messy ball just one more time. He places a hand over mine, and my twitching fingers lie still.

'For the price of one of these cakes we could stop off at a supermarket and buy several large bars of Dairy Milk.'

I am glad that we parked in the dark end of the car park, there are no admonishments here for wanting to play with a wick.

I'd have a fancy laptop bag instead of a backpack that made me look like an adult still doing Duke of Edinburgh Award . . .

I come home from work, stressed, and pull my laptop out to continue working long into the evening.

42

He hands me a glass of red as I click close on an irritating pop-up telling me that my iCloud storage is full and that everything needs updating. I sip the red wine, wishing I could either learn to like it or have the confidence to admit I think it tastes like rust.

He rubs my shoulders and tells me all the stress will be worth it when I get the promotion over stupid Rob with the big ears. Finally, nearing midnight, I close the laptop. 'Done,' I say, flicking him a knowing look. 'Shall we retire to bed?'

'I think I will stay up a little longer,' he says, surprising me. I go to bed feeling hurt and alone: rejected. I spitefully coil myself into the duvet knowing that once I'm asleep it would take a legion to wrench it from my iron grasp, and he will have to sleep feeling ever so slightly chilly. Serves him right.

The next day when I open my laptop I am filled with remorse for my actions: all my apps have been updated and there are two free gigabytes of data in my iCloud. No more pop-ups for at least a month. Well, not on the computer anyway . . .

If we were married I'd practically be Nigella Lawson . . .

I emerge from the kitchen after hours of sweat, tears and pastry. I place the dishevelled pie on the table in front of him.

'It's not very good,' I say, looking at my culinary disaster, secretly hoping it tastes more Michelin-star than it looks. It looks pretty Michelin tyre.

He looks up at me, seeing the hours and the work I have put in. He smiles kindly.

'No, it's not,' he confirms, 'but it's your first time. You cannot expect to be good your first time.'

'I know something I was good at first time,' I say coyly, and the pie is abandoned in favour of a rough puff elsewhere.

April, May

'When he fills the car up with fuel he always manages to stop on a round number.'

We'd be getting ready to host the party of a lifetime . . .

'The cake looks nothing like a unicorn,' I say despairingly, eyeing the lumpen pink nar-donkey I have created. It looks nothing like the BBC Good Food website promised it would, even though I have faithfully followed every single one of the instructions I understood.

Klipp's second birthday party begins in four hours and I am beside myself.

'She's going to be so upset.' I promised myself I would never cry over baking unless I actually was selected for *The Great British Bake Off* (the series where Mel and Sue make a triumphant return, of course) and so I try to tell myself that the tears now springing to my eyes are definitely a result of the pregnancy hormones. I have heard they can hang around for up to eighteen years after you give birth.

He is also assessing the unicorn cake. His eyes – so often reserved for gazing at me adoringly – are now critiquing my attempt at a cake.

'You are right,' he declares into the tense kitchen. 'It looks nothing like a unicorn.'

I deflate. I've let him down. I've let Klipp down. I've let us all down. He is so good at everything he turns a hand to, but here I am, in a stained apron with pink icing in my hair, having failed. He looks up at me and continues, 'But unicorns do not, and have never, existed, and therefore do not look like anything except as dictated by the human imagination. So, while this cake looks nothing like a unicorn, it also looks *exactly* like a unicorn.'

My mind does mental gymnastics trying to understand how he has managed both to lift my spirits and teach me baking philosophy at once. I am overcome with a burning desire to do some physical gymnastics too. On him.

The guests are due to start arriving in an hour. The buffet is laid out across the trestle table in the conservatory ready for bacteria-ridden fingers to get stuck into. Balloons are nestling against each other, tied to the garden fence on ribbons. The house is the absolute picture of what Pinterest assures me is 'domestic perfection'. We have spent an obscene amount of time, money and effort on a party for a person too young to even comprehend the concept of ageing. I'm not sorry.

Meanwhile, I'm upstairs trying to convince said two-year-old that she cannot die from having her hair brushed. (They never show this part on Pinterest.) She is flailing her tiny yet genetically superior arms at me and demanding I let her attend the party with a flossy nest instead of bunches.

'Come on sweetheart,' I coax, trying to remember everything my 800 parenting blogs have taught me about her temper being a product of frustration at the world. *She's not a spoiled, temperamental, rabid monster*, I repeat to myself, *she's a unique genius in the body of a two-year-old.*

'Mummy brushes her hair – look, it's not hurting at all.' I run the brush through my own hair to show her and am alarmed by how much of it seems to be coming out. I wonder if my hair's reluctance to stay on my head is down to the brushing or the stress of having a daughter.

My husband appears in the doorway and surveys the situation with a managerial eye.

'I do not brush my hair,' he says. I fall back on my heels, dumbstruck at him swiping my legs out from underneath me. This is not the way Sue's Sugar and Screen-free Organic Co-Parenting Guide suggested we work.

'Daddy is being silly . . .' I say to Klipp, trying to laugh it off.

'I am not being silly and my name is not Daddy,' he says, fully entering the room. It might be my imagination, but it seems to brighten. He sits on the edge of Klipp's tiny bed. 'I do not brush my hair, Klipp. Because my hair is very short.' From behind his back he pulls out his stainless steel clippers. 'Perhaps if you don't want to have your hair brushed, it is because you want to have short hair like mine?'

He switches the clippers on and they buzz menacingly in his hands. My body convulses as I think back to the last, and very different time, I saw him sat on a bed with something buzzing in his hand.

Klipp looks horrified and dashes into my arms, ready to be coiffered for the party. He switches off the clippers and stands up. So tall against the miniature furniture.

'Good decision. No clippers for Klipp,' he says, and then chuckles at his joke. He is magnificent. My lengthy comment beneath Sue's Sugar and Screen-free Organic Co-Parenting Guide will not be the only outpouring of passion under our roof tonight.

The party is in full swing. Sugar rampages through bloodstreams inside children. Children stampede through what once was my home but is now an adventure playground furnished by Habitat. In the Rorschach of sticky fingerprints on the patio doors, I'm convinced I can see my mother's disapproving face. The condensation from my glass of lemonade cools my clammy palms as I school my face into a serene expression. I have been practising this for weeks in the mirror. It is vital that every fibre of my being emanates the message 'My home was not complete until it was ruined by a pack of wild middle-class children. Their joyous happiness is more important than my carpets or sanity.'

The other parents seem taken in by my performance. This party has been carefully planned to be the second-best child's party each of them has been to, conceding greatness only to their own precious offspring's celebrations.

Suddenly I am cornered by two parents who are insistent that we discuss the academic attainment of our respective progeny. I try to join in, but struggle to

51

know or care what a phonic is and whether or not Klipp should be eating them. I feel my thin veneer of parental perfection wearing thin; soon these two vultures will realise I am a sham and will laugh at me from the front of their Range Rovers all the way home.

But I am rescued by my knight in shining track-suit, who is marching out to the garden with a ball under his arm. The children surround him and within minutes he has the attention of everyone at the party. He is at once spine-tinglingly good with the children and excessively impressive with his feet. He plays with them for a full half-an-hour, twenty minutes longer than could reasonably have been anticipated, and then makes his way back into the house.

As he passes me, I wink and say, 'Impressive ball skills.'

Quick as a flash he shoots back, 'I prefer my wife's.' Just loud enough for our contemporaries to know that the passion is still alive in our marriage.

Later that night we are surrounded by the debris of the party. The guests have long since fled and the house is a cheerful shambles; our infant Gatsby asleep upstairs. We are entwined on the sofa down-stairs, watching the latest Scandinavian crime drama. Watching it gives me a powerful urge to paint the hall in greys and blues. I begin scrolling the Farrow & Ball website. On screen a blond man is stood in a field of corn scrutinising a flat horizon and an impossibly graphic strangulation. It makes me yearn for the simpler times of Jonathan Creek.

'I don't understand what's going on,' I muse quietly, enjoying the faint smell of sweat from my beloved's body.

'That's because you keep looking at your phone instead of watching the programme,' he says sharply. It is the perfect end to a perfect day.

We'd read several papers over breakfast, and I'd probably have grown-up taste buds that didn't think coffee tasted mean . . .

Adele is in the paper for having lost a lot of weight. I stare at the pictures wishing I liked the way I look.

'I never seem to be able to lose weight,' I complain loudly, taking a bite of buttery toast. 'I've tried everything.'

'You have tried everything except burning more calories than you consume,' he replies.

Later I show him my favourite way to exercise.

We'd visit garden centres together as a legitimate weekend activity . . .

Despite much careful planning, and many stern words with myself on the way to the garden centre, I still manage to completely forget I am not Capability Brown. There amongst the rows of dripping foliage I am filled with the utmost confidence that any plant will thrive beneath my careful touch. Never mind that I have killed even the most basic leaves to cross my threshold; the easy-to-comprehend labels on these plants assure me that my garden will be a bountiful delight if I only take them up on their very generous three-for-two offer. It's inconsequential that the more attention I pay to a plant the more it wilts. I may very well have the complete opposite of green fingers (red toes?), but that is only because I have so far not spent enough money on products to improve myself.

Under the yellow strip lighting, with the smell of warm soil drifting by, I'm amazed I've never noticed how easy it would be to become a full-time gardener before. Of course my back wouldn't ache if I had the right ergonomically designed copper trowel. Of course I would barely get any mud under my finger-nails if I owned these lightweight, breathable gloves (reversible with two patterns to match any gardening overalls).

It would be shortsighted not to take both the French and dwarf lavenders so in they both go, and really if I'm going to have one fuchsia then I need the one in the opposite colour scheme to set it off or it's all been for naught. Before I know it I am accepting awards at Kew for having the bold, brash audacity to place broad-leaved plants against a climbing wisteria.

Obviously, plants are just the beginning. All I would need to do is look into purchasing the neighbours' garden and knocking down the dividing fence and I would be able to buy this wooden pirate ship climbing frame for Klipp too. It has a fully working plank and steering wheel! She may develop up to no motor skills or imagination without it.

I have been browsing the packets of vegetable seeds for some time, delighted by the prospect of being able to feed Klipp a diet of entirely homegrown, organic produce within four-to-six weeks, when my husband returns from finding the Cuprinol and stares at the trolley aghast.

'You are trying to be the *Ground Force* again I see?' he says, his irresistible eyebrow raised. I glance sheepishly at my trolley full of dreams.

'I really like the idea of getting into gardening,' I say.

'Of course you do,' he intones kindly. 'You are standing in a room designed by experts to make you like the idea of gardening. However, prior to arriving in this place you have never shown any inclination to play around in mud and nor will you once you leave.'

Suddenly the rose-tinted spectacles fall from my eyes, along with the tulip- and begonia-tinted pairs, and I see the trick for which I have fallen. My beloved stands before me – showing me the path through this leafy temptation. There are protruding buds on more than just the roses.

'I'll put it all back,' I say, scooping up an ambitiously large chrysanthemum and replacing it on its shelf.

'All of it?' he says, in a teasingly enticing voice. My interest is piqued.

'Was there something you liked the look of?' I reply, hoping it's the peony.

'I like the sound of the bedding plants,' he says with a wink, and turns towards the till. His monthly joke is delivered effortlessly and thrills the crowd of one.

I'd be inconsolable from smashing a job interview for an entry-level role and yet, inexplicably, not being offered the position of CEO there and then instead . . .

'I didn't get the job,' I say, my eyes brimming with tears. He looks at me and puts out a hand to hold mine.

'You would have been so good at it. But if you didn't get it, you can't have been the best candidate.'

Wow, I think. I hadn't believed I could feel worse.

'And if you were that good and didn't get it, just think how good you're going to be at the job for which you are the best candidate.'

That night I am the best candidate for rock-solid dick.

He'd come home after a hard day's football managing . . .

He sits down heavily on the bed, pulling his socks from his weary feet. His feet are good, despite him being a big man.

'These socks have a hole in,' he says, and then takes them and throws them into the bin. Straight away. Like, there and then. After putting that one away so early, he finds very little resistance to any of his further shots on goal.

I'd have special dungarees and one of those 1950s hair ribbons for when I did housework . . .

I am sorting through the detritus in the loft, trying to make some space for slightly newer detritus. I have a very clear filing system for the loft: it contains things that I no longer need or want but that fill me with an unspecified melancholic guilt when I think about throwing them away.

Old photo albums are boxed near furniture that I keep intending to spruce up but never do, as for some reason the new television shows people keep making are always more interesting than sanding old chairs in the front garden. Ornaments that were never very ornamental slumber within the very same bubble wrap in which they entered this house. There is an entire cardboard box dedicated to things that might come in handy again one day – they have been in that box for close to eight years. I sometimes wonder what I think might happen, that hasn't happened in the previous eight years, for which I could suddenly need a watering can that plays 'Frosty the Snowman'.

My husband itches to come up here and just take the whole world of crap to the recycling centre. But this is my domain, my cave of chaos that his logic and lack of sentimentality cannot infiltrate. This is probably why it is the worst room in the entire house.

'Perhaps you might need a hand,' he calls from downstairs. I can hear a note of frustration in his voice. The out-of-place box on the landing is beginning to get to him. I'll make it up to him with a different box later.

'No, I'm fine,' I call back, breezily. And I am fine. I am surrounded by comforting nonsenses and the memories woven into them. My wedding dress lounges against the wall in its soft bag. I unzip the case a little way and breathe in the scent of the material – it smells of stale wine, sweat and dust. I remember the look on his face as he saw me coming down the aisle in it. The way he leant in and whispered in my ear when I reached him. 'You look beautiful,' he said, 'But you know, I'd have married you in a bin bag. Then we could have put this money towards a house deposit.'

I smile at the memory. Thinking of our wedding night, all those many years ago, when he showed me the size of his ISA.

'This is the greatest day of my life,' he'd said. I have thanked the stars since then that we married before 1 June 2019.

Back in the present day I find the bag I was searching for. It contains a collection of Klipp's vests and baby-gros from her newborn days, which I am giving to a friend who is due to give birth any day now. I think it will be good for Klipp to not get into the habit of having a large bag of clothes in the house that she will never fit into again.

I toss the bag down through the hatch, and squash the other boxes further back to make space for their new cellmate. I climb down and lift the new box, once again guiltily eyeing the collection of outgrown soft toys. Closing the hatch, I descend the ladder in a mist of that distinctive sadness that comes from being able to touch objects from the past, but not the past itself.

My husband carries the bag of Klipp's old clothes out to the car. 'Are you ok?' he asks, concerned at my unusually distracted demeanour. I am not normally this quiet unless I am extremely hungry or angry. Or the latter due to the former.

'Yes, yes I'm fine – just a bit misty-eyed at all the things in the loft.' I smile reassuringly.

'You are not confusing *Toy Story* for a documentary again?' He raises one cheek into a teasing grin.

He makes me laugh and we close the boot together. I lean into his chest – enjoying his strength and the warmth radiating from the polyester. 'I am very proud that under my management Liverpool won the UEFA Champions League Final against Tottenham Hotspur with a 2–0 result on the 1 June 2019', he says, and I sigh as the conversation makes its way immediately back to football. He has more though, 'But I prefer to watch the training videos of my up-and-coming squad than replays of that match. We will always have won the UEFA Champions League Final against Tottenham Hotspur with a 2–0 result on the 1 June 2019 and that was exciting but, also, it is a finite event. The dreams I have when I watch the training videos though, and I think of us winning future titles: there is limitless glory there. I cannot win another trophy by asking the boys to repeat the game in which we won the last one. Yes, you are giving away a bag of clothes that Klipp will not wear again, but she did wear them and we will never lose that. Now you can dream of all the clothes she has yet to wear: her first school uniform, her prom dress, some random thing you have bought with her on a whim in the Debenhams Blue Cross

Sale, her graduation robes, her wedding dress. It is all still to come, and you will miss it if you are always looking at the things she has taken off.'

By the time he finishes speaking my cheeks are wet with tears and my . . . well, you can finish that one off yourself, as I do later.

If we were together I'd be a real morning person . . .

'The neighbours are having an extension put on!' I exclaim, furious at being woken up at the crack of dawn by the sound of hammering.

'I know,' he says, already halfway through his morning yoga. He is the ultimate Warrior II.

'They could have given us some warning,' I scowl, peeking out from between the curtains at the yammering workmen. 'How did you know they were having it done?'

He slides gracefully into Downward Dog. The yoga mat is sluttily submissive beneath him. 'I read the notices for planning permission pinned to the lamp posts.'

I've always wondered what those odd pieces of paper from the council were. It has never occurred to me that anybody would stop to look at them. My admiration for the way he interacts with the adult world shoots up. I have to hope that the builders outside drown out the sound of our own hammering.

We'd have a big garden with a water feature that was genuinely nice, and when people commented on how nice it all was I'd be all like 'Oh I barely touch it - we're lucky really it was like this when we moved in . . .'

It's the first properly hot day . . . Late into May, England has woken up to a fierce heat emanating from a radiant blue sky. I am stretched out in the garden, feeling the warm rays of the sun massaging my winter tensions away.

Suddenly, the sun is not the only thing stroking my bare skin. He is behind me, casting a cool shadow.

'How long have you been out here?' he asks, running a lazy hand up and down my back. I shiver with delight.

'Nearly an hour,' I murmur, thoroughly enjoying where this is going.

'Then you need to reapply,' he says, squirting out the recommended two milligrams per square centimetre of skin of factor thirty. He rubs gently, making sure the lotion is partially absorbed, but still fully visible on the skin in order to form an adequate barrier to ultraviolet rays. I do have one place, however, that needs him to apply no extra cream.

I'd have a cupboard for everything and not just shove things behind the sofa when tidying . . .

I look around at the mess in the living room, despairing at its ability to generate clutter every time my back is turned.

'I'd feel guilty having a cleaner though,' I agonise, picturing the look on my mother's face if she knew I was paying another woman to clean my house. 'I'm not nearly busy enough to justify having a cleaner. What kind of a message would it send to Klipp?'

'The message that you are an independent woman who can direct her funds in the manner which brings her the most happiness and efficiency?' he responds simply. His grasp of feminism is so uniquely insightful that it is simply my duty to let him grasp some of my own feminism.

I'd totally be one of those 'when life hands you lemons here's 101 ways to make your home eco-friendly using half a lemon' people . . .

I am in pieces, staring into the mirror, seeing my entire life flash before my eyes.

'It's awful,' I sob. 'I can never leave the house again. She has absolutely ruined me.'

'What is wrong?' he asks gently, his head tilted to one side. 'You wanted a fringe and you have a fringe?'

'But not like this!' I almost scream at him. 'This is a Claudia Winkleman fringe and I really wanted more of a messy Taylor Swift! It makes my jaw line so fat.'

'Hey now, calm down,' he soothes. 'You're imagining things. It is not possible for the hair at the top of your head to increase the amount of body fat at the bottom. It is most likely you always had that amount of body fat there, but the new fringe is just making you notice it.'

I moan despairingly into the mirror, 'I won't be able to leave the house for a month.'

'I think you look beautiful,' he says firmly, not brooking any of my nonsense. 'But I can see that you're upset.' Ever so gently, he reaches up and lifts one of his beloved baseball caps off the custom-made rotating hat stand. He lays it gently to rest over my ruined hair. 'There,' he says, 'I would like you any way – but perhaps now you feel a little more confident?'

How could I not feel more confident in a hat that was used to housing that mind? It's like wearing Diana's wedding dress or Mufasa's mane.

I am so overwhelmed with passion by his support that, despite having found a solution for the hair fiasco, we don't leave the house anyway. By the time we break for orange slices my fringe is messier than any hairdresser could have achieved.

I'd have one of those cool Dualit toasters and I'd make us brunch to have on a tray like in adverts about Mother's Day . . .

The toast pops out of the toaster, my knife hovers above it, waiting to punish the soft white tile with some slippery spread. I am ravenous.

I hear his voice floating through from the front room. 'Laura, if you even think about eating that in bed and spreading crumbs everywhere then you will be sleeping in the garage for the rest of the week.'

He knows me better than I know myself. I laugh, and there is only one thing I spread over the bed that day.

June, July, August

'He flicks the light switch and is the only human being on planet earth who still looks ok when the big light is on.'

I'd be the sort of person who has a stack of greetings cards already bought in a drawer and gets them prepped at the beginning of the month . . .

It's his birthday. As ever he has requested that there is minimal fuss made over the anniversary of his birth. He has expressly forbidden me to apply candles to a dessert, except in the unlikely event that he happens to turn eight again. He has promised to divorce me if I ever throw him a surprise party.

It singes the edges of my very soul not to be allowed to shower him with all the affection I would like to. He is the king. He is the Boss. He is very, very sensible. I would build him statues, I would name train stations after him, I would write him novels. But I understand doing that would be for me, not him.

I hand him his gift and worry all over again that I haven't put in enough effort. However, the look on his face as he opens it and beams at his new

Rawlplugs and Deep Heat is all I need to feel like I'm part-woman, part-soda stream.

I'd have the nervous flop sweat getting ready to go and pitch for a job I really wanted . . .

I have another interview today. I'm trying to be positive, but I am nervous. Going part-time with my career while Klipp is young has made me feel insecure.

'You will be magnificent,' says a deep voice my body recognises. I turn to see its owner leaning casually against the door frame, observing me.

I am embarrassed, unable to absorb the compliment, so instead I deflect by smoothing down my well-ironed dress.

'Oh, I don't know about that. At my last interview everyone in there was ten years younger than me. I feel like a dinosaur. I bet none of them have children either.' It has been harder and harder to look interviewers in the eye and tell them where I see myself in five years. They want me to say I will be chained to my desk in the exact spot I'd have occupied for the preceding four-and-a-half years, but I have to squash down an image of my seven-year-old defrosting her own dinner.

'So, your fear is that the people you are up against have no other responsibilities and are younger than you?' He sounds confused by this and I look at him perplexed.

'Of course. If you had to choose between two . . .' I search for the word and hope that it's right '. . . strikers, and they're both equally as good, but one is younger and has no children, who would you choose?'

He is silent for a moment and I wonder if I have stumped him. Is this the day I teach him some-thing other than how to most frequently stub one's toes? But then he nods his head at his own thoughts and looks back at me.

'But, you are not interviewing to be a player. And if I were choosing a coach, or a manager – as you would be on this team, then someone with more experience who is already showing me they can balance two equally important worlds would be a huge tick from me. The fact that the love of their life, their own child was at home, and they missed them deeply, yet still had the urge to be out at a job, being productive and being themselves . . . well, that would show me that the job was part of their identity, beyond just a pay cheque. I think that is also a huge bonus.'

He finishes his speech and I realise I have grasped my hands to my chest with delight at his stirring words. I can see why the journalists clamour for his press conferences. I can only hope that their follow-up questions are not as rigorous as the ones my body is asking of him.

We'd be going to Holland & Barrett to buy protein powder in the One Penny Sale . . .

It's a beautiful Sunday afternoon: bright blue skies and a high sun. The morning's rain has conveniently washed the streets clear of leftovers from weekend revellers. There's neither a piss stain nor a carroty noodle-splatter in sight.

We're strolling down the high street, holding hands, our fingers interlocked as we pass Boots. I'm enjoying the sensation of his warm palm when, suddenly, his hand slips out of mine and he is behind me in an instant. I catch my breath and turn to him, 'What are you doing?'

'There are people coming the other way,' he says, staring grimly into the distance, 'It would be irresponsible to block the pavement.' Later that night I find him behind me again.

When we had people round, we'd have enough chairs for everyone to sit on without having to bring out a computer chair . . .

It is 3.45 p.m. and the entire extended family is due round in an hour for a barbecue we can't remember why we offered to throw. We are still in Sainsbury's playing a very dull version of Supermarket Sweep where the aim isn't to win a holiday, but to create a menu that can simultaneously please a coeliac, a lactose intolerant, a vegan and a boomer.

I fling three packets of chicken wings into the trolley. He catches my arm gently and twirls me towards him. I squash down visions of him winning *Strictly Come Dancing* to try to focus on what he's saying.

'Hey, why have you got three packets? Two will be plenty.' He goes to lift one back out of the trolley and put it back.

'They're on offer,' I say, indicating the harsh yellow label blaring savings into the fluorescent light of the store.

'But we do not need three packets, and this offer only actually saves us 12p. We should save the fridge space for things with a longer shelf life.'

The shiver down my spine has nothing to do with the chiller aisle.

We arrive home to find out that half the guests are coming earlier than planned, half are coming later and the only person we were really excited to see has unfortunately had to cancel. The drizzle that was supposed to have ceased an hour ago is just sputtering its last spiteful drops out over the garden. The garden *and* my mackintoshed husband. He is stood in a raincoat and shorts beneath an umbrella stoking the barbecue to life with mesmerising efficiency. It's the perfect merge of our two cultures. I find I am marinating more than just the legs of a chicken.

Ninety minutes later, the table is piled high with delicious-looking treats. I have made coleslaw from scratch, prepared two quiches – one meaty, one vegetarian – buttered bread rolls, prepared two different types of salads and conjured a quick dressing to accompany them, sliced different cheeses, mixed a jug of sangria, opened the red, found a cooler for the white, prepared juice for the children and non-drinkers, and gathered the cutlery and plates. I sit down in my chair just as my husband brings across the large platter of meats from the barbecue.

'Oh it must be lovely to have a man who does all the cooking for you,' says my mother, gazing up at him adoringly. The meat is cooked to perfection, but it cannot shake the bitter taste from my mouth.

The family gorges – a happy plague of locusts descending on a red gingham tablecloth. When we are satiated, my husband is the first out of his chair to start removing dishes to the kitchen. My mother's hand shoots out to stay him.

'Oh, no – you've done enough. Sit down.' She eyes me meaningfully, and I sigh and stand up to start gathering utensils.

He remains on his feet though, plates still in hand.

'I don't find doing it to be a burden,' he says, continuing to stack them. 'I would rather clean up than watch my wife do it alone.' He smiles across the table and it curls over Mum's head landing hard in my open goal mouth.

'Well, you're very sweet to help Laura,' my mother mutters, not enjoying the exchange.

'I am not helping her,' he smiles at her. 'Helping would be to imply it is her job and I am assisting. We are just doing it together.'

My mother is silent. Even the birds fall still in awe of him. If you were to listen carefully though you would be able to hear the faint beating of my ovaries.

We'd have the sort of relationship where no subject would be off-limits, no matter how difficult . . .

'I'd like to get a dog,' I say to him, 'to help with my anxiety. I've been thinking about it all morning and researching how having a pet can help to keep people calm.' He looks over at me, his iPad still blaring with the last notes of that song about always having someone to walk home with.

'That is a lot of pressure to put on a dog's shoulders,' he says. 'Do you not think it would be fairer to approach a medical professional first?'

We'd have a team approach to managing domestic issues . . .

This week has already gone on for approximately 428 days and it is only Tuesday. I crash onto the sofa, furious with the world.

'I don't know what to make for dinner – I've run out of ideas and will to live,' I snap, despairingly. He looks over mildly from his position in the armchair, and then slides a sheet of A3 paper out from under his work papers.

'It is a good job I prepared this meal planner of nutritionally balanced lunches and dinners for the rest of the month, isn't it?'

As my eyes scan the colour-coded day planner, complete with cooking times and calorie content, my stomach is not the only empty growler.

I'd look at myself in a compact mirror and then say, 'Gosh, I must just go and freshen up' even though I looked like I'd literally just stepped out of a salon . . .

We are off to the airport today for our first trip abroad together since Klipp was born. She is not coming with us and this either makes me a strong modern feminist inspired by Kate Middleton, or a hollow shark-eyed Nazi who only had a child as a fashion accessory. It all depends which 'What Kind of Mother Are You?' *Cosmo* questionnaire you read.

I'm not a keen traveller. It's not a fear of flying so much as a fear of losing paperwork and holding up queues. There is no paranoia quite like the paranoia that perhaps you *are* a terrorist, but you just didn't know until you joined this security line.

Admittedly, since beginning to travel with my darling beau, I have found a lot of the weight lifted from my shoulders. Literally and figuratively. No-one wields a seventy-five-litre suitcase like my man. He always manages to find us the very best price thanks to his extensive spreadsheet that compares the most competitive deals across several different independent, family-owned travel companies. He shows me the formula he's using to work out which is the best, and I see a pride in his eyes that's usually reserved for Klipp. I wonder if he had as much fun making the spreadsheet as he had making Klipp . . . probably affirmative.

We arrive at the airport bang-on two hours before departure, and he has already checked us in online with a swipe of his tanned finger. I have never wanted to be an iPhone more.

As we head towards security I panic, searching through my bag for a lip balm that I absolutely know I put in there but cannot find now. Just as my frustration peaks I turn to look at him, and there he is . . .

'Lip balm is a gel,' he says simply, holding up a clear plastic bag. 'I have moved all your liquids to these bags for expediency at the conveyor belt.' Later that day, it's me who is efficient at the belt.

We board the plane and I am struggling to lift my bag into the overhead locker. I've already had to wander up and down the aisle three times trying to find a gap. I'm holding up the plane. We will miss our runway slot and hit bad weather and die all because I didn't get in the boarding queue quick enough. I suspect the flight attendant is trying to frown at me because there is a small crack forming in the foundation on her forehead. Sweat soaks into my elastic-waisted travelling trousers. Suddenly strong arms relieve me of my physical burden. The bags of strangers part before him, like Moses at the Red Sea, and my case slides effortlessly into the space he has created. He's so good at finding an opening.

We settle down for the flight, but the seats are cramped and even with the aisle seat his long legs are causing him to shift and fidget.

'I can't get comfortable,' he complains.

'Perhaps there would be more room in the toilets?' I suggest, winking at him seductively. 'We could join the mile high club?'

'You are a very bad girl,' he says to me sternly. 'You should know the average cruising height of an aeroplane is between 5.9 and 7.2 miles.'

We arrive at the hotel and it is beautiful. We're a mixture of delighted to be child-free, terrified we'll hate being away from her, and terrified we won't miss her at all, so we've pushed the boat out for an ultra-romantic couples' holiday to distract ourselves. As soon as he has finished familiarising himself with the emergency exits, we head for the pool, each with a book in hand.

I notice his choice of reading material is *A Manager's Guide to Managing to Manage: Management Edition*, and I ask him, 'Don't you want something more relaxing to read?'

'What could be more relaxing than knowing I am improving?' he asks, nonplussed.

Suddenly the pool is not the wettest thing in the vicinity.

We take a sunset stroll along the beach. The palms shimmy in the light breeze; the sea laps gently up onto pale sand.

'It's beautiful, isn't it?' I say, astounded by the natural beauty.

'There is an improved quality to this light with increased red tone,' he agrees. 'Everything is better in red.'

I turn to him playfully, 'If you were stranded on a desert island, what two things would you have with you?'

He considers my question and then asks, 'Where was I going when I got stranded?'

'Er, on holiday I suppose?' I reply, unsure as to how this changes things.

'Then I would have with me the exact things I have now on this trip. I did not know I was going to become stranded.'

His logic is as faultless as his relentless attacking managerial style.

The holiday is everything I dreamed it would be. We sunbathe, patronise local restaurants, patronise locals, and soak in the culture. As the time to go home stalks closer I can feel the blues creeping up on me like a familiar ghost.

'What's the matter?' he says, somehow picking up on my inner turmoil as I sigh repeatedly and slam my clothes back into the case.

'I want to stay here. Everything is so much better here,' I say, dramatically and fling myself on the bed. Klipp would move on if I never returned, wouldn't she? It's not like I'm an iPad or anything.

'You will be just as happy when you get home. If you like swimming and reading so much then just make sure to include those in your daily routine when we get home as well.' His practicality is the lighthouse for my rocky mood.

'It wouldn't be the same,' I complain. 'There's something magical about this place – I don't want to go back to the real world.'

'This is very much the real world for the people being paid minimum wage to wait on you hand and foot,' he reminds me. He is completely right of course, there is nothing more blissful or shameful than my ignorance.

How does he always manage to show me the world in a new light? I am overwhelmed with the desire to turn out all the lights.

I'd probably be so fancy I'd shop in Waitrose and remember to take bags for life . . .

I get the shopping home from the supermarket and he carries the bag with soap powder and the wine while I pretend the one with the multipack bag of crisps is my limit. Not only does he help me bring the shopping in, he also innately understands that the shopping does not live in bags on the kitchen floor and he helps me put it away. I offer to do the freezer stuff since there is more than one set of loins to cool off.

We'd have big, intellectual conversations on a sofa not bought in the DFS sale . . .

'It's not a big deal,' I say, coming back into the room, 'It's just Louise was saying it doesn't really count as reading if you listened to the audiobook, so I wasn't sure whether or not to tick that one off.'

I drop the list of '50 Books You Should Have Read by Now' onto the coffee table with *Wuthering Heights* as yet unticked.

He pauses *Match of the Day* to frown up at me, 'Not counting audiobooks would be to say that the method of consuming the story is more important than the act of having absorbed the story. There is an argument to be made that listening to a tale is older and therefore more traditional than reading.'

I nod, slowly, 'Yes, but then is it fair to say I've also read *David Copperfield* because I watched that film of it with the *This Country* woman and the guy from *Slumdog Millionaire*?'

He ponders my point, staring at the uninteresting wall while he thinks. 'No,' he replies finally, 'because that is an adaptation whereas an audiobook is the same material in a different format.'

Match of the Day goes back on, and I wonder if anyone has ever before fantasised about banging their husband backstage at the Hay Literary Festival, to a soundtrack of Gary Lineker trying to find ten minutes of discussion in a 0–0 draw.

We'd have busy domestic weekday mornings and yoghurt over fresh fruit would magically be enough to keep us full up until lunch time . . .

'I hate doing the nursery run,' I complain to him, as I wipe Klipp's Cheerio residue off the table, floor, walls and ceiling of our kitchen. 'I don't think the other mums like me.'

He considers me from his position by the window where he is feeding his sourdough starter. The early morning sun falls across his face, his eyes are shielded by the peak of his cap, making him seem reserved, unattainable. The invisible yeast spores flock to him and his bubbling jar. How could they not?

'Why wouldn't they like you?' he asks, shaking flour out of the bag onto the weighing scales with all the precision of a surgeon.

'I don't know,' I whine, vaguely, 'I just don't seem to fit in.'

'But you are all there for the same purpose in the same situation, how could you possibly not fit in?' he says, his large hands tipping the jug of tepid

91

water to the perfect angle to let the liquid fall into the eager starter. 'I think perhaps this is all in your own mind and you are projecting your own insecurities onto the perfectly normal reactions of women too distracted by their own busy days to have time to be elaborately attentive to you.'

'Can't you just for once take my side?' I mutter, and flounce out of the house, trailing Klipp behind me because sometimes having a really sensible partner is rubbish.

When I return home that night, he still has absolutely no idea what he said wrong.

On those rare Saturdays where he wasn't overseeing the winning of some cup final or other, we would be out with our very successful, yet still fun, friends . . .

It's a swelteringly hot day. We have driven out to a pub garden to enjoy a lazy Sunday afternoon in the sun, and I breathe in that unique scent of hot, wooden, bench tables. Klipp follows a ladybird across the grass, her chubby legs sticking out of a fat nappy. Every fifteen seconds she remembers she has a hat on and tugs it off, furious. It is my job to dash across the grass and reattach the hat without breaking eye contact and losing my place in the conversation at the table. Condensation rolls down the outside of the glasses and I try to enjoy the afternoon in my split role, half-carefree adult, half-preoccupied mother.

Four adult men sit down at the table next to ours. Each one pulls a cigarette packet out of their pockets and lights up. I look down at Klipp . . . I don't want to be that parent that instantly whips their child away tutting at other people, but equally, I don't want her to have a deeper voice than me by the time she is able to speak in full sentences. Her hat goes flying into the grass and as I sweep in to reapply it, I lift her into my arms and move her to the other side of the table and out of the smoke. She moans at the loss of her red and black friend, but is more than happy to get distracted by a patch of daisies that urgently need picking. It is not long before I am scooping half-chewed petals out of her mouth with a hastily wiped finger. Each sip of my drink is warmer than the last and I glance jealously at the childless friends we are with and their responsibility-free afternoon.

'Shall I get the next round in?' asks the man of my dreams, extracting his long legs from under the bench. We nod in agreement and he disappears into the shade of the pub. I rescue a butterfly from the sticky hands of my offspring and drain the warm dregs of my wine.

A phone rings on the table next to us and one of the men stands up to take the call, moving away from his table and round to the one on the other side of ours. He sits down, and lights up another cigarette. I scowl at the man: he has now boxed us in completely with his smoke. I am unsure where to put Klipp. Perhaps he won't stay long; she will cope. I fight the urge to Google, 'How long does it take for a two-year-old to develop terminal lung cancer?' and try to join in the conversation with my friends. But I am distracted.

His conversation is clearly complicated and more drawn-out than he expected, and he pulls yet another cigarette from the packet and lights it. I despair. I imagine myself marching over and huffily lifting my child, my baby, the continuation of my DNA, the continuation of *his* DNA, from the floor and running across the grass with her to safety.

'You monster!' I would scream at the murderer in blue jeans, weeping over the smoke-stained skin of my daughter.

Perhaps I could come up with a distraction to lure him away. Maybe I could pretend to be a waitress calling him over with a question about their order. Or perhaps I could speak to the barman and have him ejected. Or even arrested. My mind whirrs with plans to remedy the solution.

My imagination is interrupted by four drinks being placed on the table by hands I recognise.

'Oh dear,' he says, glancing at the smoke on both sides of us. 'This will not do.'

I stir involuntarily against the wooden bench as I prepare to watch the lion defend his pride against the invader. Within two steps he is towering over the man on the phone. I hold my breath.

'Excuse me,' he begins, polite and calm, 'would you mind not smoking there? It's just with your friends smoking on the other side there is nowhere smoke-free to put our daughter to play.'

'Yeah, of course – sorry mate, I didn't think. No worries.' The man immediately stands up and moves further off down the garden.

Our hero returns to our table and sits down. I am agog. I don't know how he came up with the ingenious solution of having a calm, polite, adult conversation with the person he had a problem with, but it was a stroke of genius. Later on, I hope to persuade him to stroke my genius.

September, October, November, December

'He has never been tempted by an article containing fifteen things he never knew about a thing. The eighth one didn't stand a chance of shocking him.'

I'd have the kind of birthdays they have in adverts where you wake up with flawless make-up to someone opening the curtains saying 'wake up sleepy head', and your duvet cover matches the pillow cases . . .

I stare into the mirror at my drooping eyes and greying hair. It is my birthday and as a gift I have got myself some crippling self-loathing.

'I don't want to be old,' I moan, burying my decrepit face in the duvet. Apparently there are seven signs of ageing, but in the mirror just now I am sure I spotted an extra forty-three. Perhaps I should call up science and tell them – they could name a crow's foot after me.

'The only other option is to be dead,' he says, handing me a cup of tea. There is no card from him with my birthday tea: he does not approve of birthday cards. However, I am feeling petulant and insecure, so I push him on the point. 'No birthday card for me?' I whine, manipulating my face into a doleful pout.

'If you would like a birthday card there are four shoeboxes of greetings cards taking up space in the bottom of the wardrobe. We have taken those with us each time we have moved house and I have never, ever seen you look at them.'

'It just would have been nice if you had got me a card, that's all,' I sulk, wondering why a fear of being unloveable often pushes me to act completely unloveably.

'No,' he says briskly, sitting down on the plump mattress. 'Why would I waste my money on some overpriced cardboard clutter? I would only need to give you a card if I was not going to see you and, as you are my wife, I have made sure I am seeing you on your birthday. If you would prefer for me to be absent, but a card to be present, then I can arrange that.'

His no-nonsense approach to my pity-party is like strong fingers in tense muscles. I pull myself out of my nest of pillows and gloom and force myself to be positive. I know it's not easy for him to take time off – he has to give 110 per cent to the squad, so there often isn't much of him to leave on my pitch when he gets home.

'You must get dressed for your birthday treat,' he says, standing up to leave the room.

'What is my birthday treat?' I ask, interest piqued.

'Me,' he says with a wink, and it turns out I do not need to be dressed at all.

We'd have dreamy weekend lie-ins because our self-soothing child would get a healthy amount of sleep and then entertain herself quietly in her room until we went in together, in our matching pyjamas, to pick her up and take her down for breakfast . . .

It's a lazy Sunday morning and we're enjoying the early light across the pillows as we wake up together. He reaches for his glasses and then notices a damp patch on the wall opposite.

'We should do something about that,' he says, then gets dressed, drives to B&Q, buys the necessary items and deals with the problem that day. From now on the bedroom is damp for more interesting reasons.

We'd have peaceful evenings where I'd swan about the house in one of those silky dressing gowns that doesn't keep you warm and is also too slippery to stay tied up...

I linger outside Klipp's bedroom door watching a perfect scene of domesticity. She is huddled in her duvet while he is sat on the edge of the little bed. His frame looks so big compared to her tiny furniture; the book in his hands thin and colourful. She is hanging on his every word. He closes the book and ruffles her hair, kissing her goodnight before joining me in the hall.

'You didn't do the voices,' I tease.

He looks at me sternly. 'There is no need for voices if you firmly explain to the listener at the beginning that any dialogue is reported speech coming via the narrator.'

An image flashes into my mind of my no-nonsense little girl growing up to be Prime Minister. He may not do his own voices, but later on he elicits some strangled ones from me.

I'd have stylish reading glasses that I wore for online meetings and I'd learn how to do my hair in one of those fancy French hair croissant thingies . . .

I am trapped in a tunnel of panicked despair. There is nothing at all to feel positive about on the entire planet.

I have been in this online meeting for fifty-one

minutes and I have aged at an approximate rate of eleven years for every one of those minutes. I have only had this new position for two weeks and I am desperate to please, but finding it very hard to concentrate.

An online meeting is much like a regular meeting except someone's put a small mirror in front of you and you have to try to focus on whatever Iain from Marketing is saying while wondering exactly how long your face has been this weird.

'Projections for this quarter are looking . . .' waffles Iain while an entire moustache sprouts from my upper lip.

'If everyone could have a look at the scripts I sent yesterday . . .' chimes in Louise from Content, but I can't see the scripts because I have the smallest, piggiest eyes a human has ever had.

Iain puts himself on mute to take a sip of his coffee. I'm lost in a world of horror as I tilt my head back to slurp my own drink and see the vista of new chins that have formed beneath my face. I feel like an explorer cresting a mountain and seeing the unconquered hills with a mixture of pride and despair at their enormity.

'What are your thoughts?' asks Joe. But I have

forgotten what I do for a living because I cannot listen and see my own face at the same time.

The meeting comes to an end and I close the laptop to trap this crone masquerading as my reflection against the keyboard.

'What's wrong with me?' I moan, face pressed desperately up against the wood of the table.

'Your meeting was not a positive experience?' asks my husband, entering the room and bringing with him the gentle scent of wood polish and freshly cut grass. How can one beard smell of so much?

'The meeting was fine, but why can't I concentrate when my own face is on the screen? I'm like a bloody budgerigar. What's wrong with me?'

'Nothing,' he declares confidently. 'You have had meetings with these people often but you have never had meetings with yourself. It is natural, then, that you should find your own face in a work environment new and therefore engaging.'

I consider his point. It is one of the only times I've ever seen my face outside of a bathroom mirror or a still photo.

He smiles at me, happy to see me appeased. 'I

would be distracted too if I was trying to work and could see your face.'

'Oh!' I shoot back, grinning. 'You prefer it when you can't see my face, do you . . .?'

'Too far, Laura. You have taken the joke too far.' He removes his coffee from beneath the machine and leaves the room. Later that night, however, he provides energetic evidence in support of my thesis.

We'd have cosy nights in watching foreign-language films that won niche awards at those arty awards ceremonies . . .

I flounce into the lounge, and throw myself onto the sofa.

'What's the matter?' he says, used to my performative strops.

'I can't think of anything to make for dinner.

There's nothing to eat in the whole house,' I whine, ignoring the perfectly serviceable jars of sauce and bags of pasta in the cupboard. 'Not a bite to eat. Maybe we should get takeaway?'

I look up through heavily mascara'd eyelashes, checking to see how my scene is going down with the audience. If I were one of his players, he would be beckoning a stretcher for me, only to have me jog back on at peak fitness thirty seconds later.

He considers me for a second, allowing me a moment to revel gloriously in my sofa-based lime-light. He puts his book to one side.

'Laura, if you want to order a takeaway then you are a grown woman, you can just say you want to order a takeaway.'

'But I don't want to order a takeaway.' I mope my mouth into a downward curve, hoping it's more Scarlett Johansson pout than 1920s French clown. 'Choosing a takeaway is almost more stressful than cooking.'

'Laura,' he raises an eyebrow, 'sometimes you are completely ridiculous.'

We look at the delivery options together. In nature everything is a delicate balance, and the same is true for choosing takeaway. It's a challenging equation: delivery time x cost / whether or not you actually want to eat it + restaurant hygiene rating = what you end up eating. I really want Chinese food, but it never works for two people. I don't want a burger, but it would be here in fifteen minutes, so maybe I do? I could murder a kebab, but is that ok to admit as a sober adult with other options?

He lifts the laptop away from me and gives me that serious look I can't resist. 'Laura, I will narrow it down to three options, and then you can just choose one of those.'

He has come up with the perfect solution. He offers Thai, Lebanese or sushi, and the moment he limits my choices I know what I want.

It is hours before a scooter delivers us a mediocre pizza. In the meantime, he finds a way to satiate my other appetites.

We'd discuss finances instead of just letting important letters pile up unopened by the front door in case they're scary inside . . .

The kitchen needs to be redecorated. For months I have been dreaming of the day I get the kitchen of my fantasies, complete with copper taps and a stylish central island. There will be no clutter once the kitchen is redesigned. We'll have a self-loading dishwasher, an oven that comes fully stocked with ideas for meals and a metallic bowl full of fruits that Klipp prefers to KitKats. Perhaps a fridge that knows when there isn't much milk left and tells you and Apple Inc.. I am ecstatic with joy that the day has finally come for me to start the planning.

But after forty-five minutes comparing quotes, I feel like a hole has opened up in my stomach lining and my joy is draining out through it. Why does this always happen? I save up for something specific and then lose all faith that it is worth it the second there are no obstacles in my way.

'It's a lot of money,' I mumble, ashen-faced. His business-savvy eye scans the quotes.

'It is,' he agrees. 'But, it is money we have.'

'Perhaps we should try and do some of it ourselves to keep the costs down?' I offer. I must admit, I do not mind the thought of him in a tool belt. He looks at me, confused.

'Do you want to do decorating?' I know that he already knows the answer to this question. I have never shown any interest in doing anything that required us using a ladder. Although I do not mind being beneath him.

'No, I just wonder if we ought to try and save a little if we can?'

He shrugs, 'We can either spend our money or our time, and I know I value two of my days extremely highly.' He continues brewing coffee, leaving me floating in the wake of his intelligence. How have I never thought of money in this way before? I hire some decorators and instantly decide how I will spend the two days we have bought ourselves.

I'd be getting glammed up to go out for the night to a swanky gala or whatever the football Oscars is . . .

The woman in the YouTube video sweeps her hand gracefully from left to right, and a perfect black line appears. It elegantly frames her beautiful almond-shaped eye, doubling its apparent size and her beauty. I lift my wand to my own eye and mimic her actions perfectly, creating a wiggly black smudge that inexplicably has a break midway before blotching out into a messy puddle in the cavernous wrinkles I seemingly just developed.

'Fuck it,' I exclaim, lifting a cotton pad to my eye to remove the offending graffiti and start again.

We are getting ready to go to a fancy dinner. Well, I am getting ready; I have waxed everything, bleached what I can't bring myself to wax, squeezed my curves into underwear that makes curves rigid, and selected a dress specially designed by a series of experts to persuade red-blooded males that they could have sex with a woman over twenty-five without vomiting. I have been between the bathroom and the bedroom for the best part of four hours preparing. Twenty minutes before we are due to leave my husband will go to the effort of choosing which colour length of silk to tie loosely around his neck, and we will appear at the party looking somehow like we have made the same amount of effort with our appearance.

I am nervous. These events make me feel giddy and sick because I'll have to make small talk and try to fit in in a room where I feel like an outsider.

'Are you nearly ready?' He appears in the door carrying a freshly ironed shirt on a hanger.

'No I'm not. I'm not nearly bloody ready. Do I look nearly bloody ready?' The words come screeching out of my mouth before I can stop them. Fear kicks off my fight-or-flight, but the irony of it all is that I am fighting the one person to whom I want to cling.

He sighs deeply. 'You are not looking forward to going?'

I instantly want to cry, or at the very least stop lashing out. 'No,' I say, keeping my words monosyllabic to give myself the best chance of keeping the tears in. It would be a shame to cry now and ruin the black line I have finally managed to draw. I briefly wonder if there is potential in a fashion where you only have to wear eye make-up on the side of your face that comes naturally to your dominant hand? Feels like the sort of thing Tilda Swinton could make fashionable.

'What is making you nervous?' he says, his gentle tone enraging me. Does he not realise these are not 'nerves'? This is not normal anxiousness? This is absolute terror. This is the big one. This party could be the end of days.

'I don't want to make small talk with new people,' I say, and it sounds so small. The fears that loom so large when they're tormenting me in my mind have spitefully metamorphosed into petty, hollow-sounding peeves now they are loose in the air. Fears that swore to me they were apocalyptic now waggle their tongues back in my direction as I imagine them landing on someone else where they weigh several tonnes less than my terror promised.

'Are you worried they will find you too interesting?' he says, removing his t-shirt to put on the crisp, white shirt.

I smile at his attempts to defrost my fear.

'I don't know what I'm worried about,' I say, feeling the muscles up my spine relax and sag as I give in to my honesty.

'Well, to know how to play today we must look at our previous performances,' he says, applying the logic that has earned him an impressive cabinet of silverware.

'I feel inadequate,' I admit. 'I second-guess every word I want to say and I worry that I'm boring to everyone I talk to.' The tears that have been threatening my clumpy mascara leak out uninvited and I am desolate.

'Do you think I am a good manager?' he asks me, throwing my thoughts off course with this question. I ponder, picturing him on the side lines hugging his team after a goal.

'Of course,' I say, not needing more than a second to think.

'And what is the main job of a manager?' he continues, gently. This I cannot answer instantly. I am confident it is something to do with the phrase 'at the end of the day', but beyond that the details of his working life are not my area of expertise. Thankfully, he is not waiting for me to respond. 'I choose the team,' he informs me. 'I select the best people and then I get the best out of them. You are the person I chose for my own team. You are the best. So, if you feel unsupported out there on the pitch then we must change the formation.'

He wipes away my tears with his words and then dominates a Full Windsor. At the party that night he barely leaves my side, and when he does, I know his eyes will find a gap in the crowd through which to meet mine if I need them. In every conversation I am introduced as a woman of substance and interest; he finds ways to include me in subjects where I would never normally find a foothold. Strong fingers are interlaced with mine whenever I feel my hands trembling with nerves. Every anecdote I tell has a smile or a laugh waiting for it at the end to lift my confidence into the next one. When we return home, we hit the showers happy.

After I'd had my hair cut, when the hairdresser asked 'Would you like to book another appointment?' I'd say, 'Yes please, I have my life together and can plan more than a few weeks in advance . . .

It's Klipp's nursery Christmas Fair this afternoon and I have spent the entire morning attempting to make something to contribute so that I don't come across like a bad mother.

It's my first experience of this unpleasant world of competitive parenting as Klipp only started nursery in the autumn and I skipped the harvest festival due to harvest time being irrelevant in the modern world.

The Christmas Fair is a curious mix of communism and capitalism: everyone must labour equally to create items that nobody wants and then we bring them all together in the village hall to sell to each other. You are the winner if you laboured the longest and spent the most.

I only remembered about the Christmas Fair at

9 a.m. because they have scheduled it for the 1 December. Scheduling events on the first of the month is a cruel and unusual punishment for people like myself who do not flip their Family Organisers over to December until the first day of December. It does explain why there was such a large herd of trestle tables at the village hall when I dropped Klipp off this morning.

Instead of spending my morning harmlessly flicking through Netflix and telling myself it's important for my job to keep abreast of current popular television shows, I am hastily trying to weave wreaths together from pipe cleaners, ribbons and the other expensive trash I could find at the craft store. I have spent close to £40 on landfill produce to make these with and I will have to price them at under £1 each in order to not be laughed out of town. If I were on *The Apprentice* I would be a meme before the show had finished airing.

A wayward glittery pipe springs out of its pleat and I wonder whether I could get away with just never returning to pick Klipp up. Would it be less effort to just have a new baby and start again?

Should I be worried about how often I consider my child coping without me?

'Oh cool, you are making festive . . . birds' nests?' My ever-supportive spouse appears at my shoulder and eyes the mess on the table.

'They are Christmas wreaths to sell at Klipp's nursery's fair this afternoon,' I snap, trying to glue a bell to a plastic star and succeeding only in gluing my thumb to my index finger.

'You are going to try and sell these?' He sounds surprised. Or worried. Possibly he is both: surprised I am going to try to sell them and then worried about me that I think this could be possible.

'Well . . . I know they're not great, but I didn't have much time, or talent, and I need to take something to sell . . .' I peter out, my excuses as weak as my crafting.

'Why do you have to take something?'

'To raise money for the nursery.'

'We pay fees for the nursery.' He sounds perplexed.

'Well, yes, but I suppose this raises money for little extras for them.' I hadn't really questioned why I was doing this, I just didn't want to look bad.

'So, we pay for our daughter to go somewhere and do crafts with people but while she is there doing crafts with people you are sitting here doing crafts alone to raise money for our daughter to do crafts somewhere else?'

As ever his summary of the hoops I am jumping through is succinct and cutting. I put down the glue, but my fingers remain sticky.

When we played board games we'd look like the families on the boxes do: all laughing at how much more fun moving plastic pieces around a board is than watching TV . . .

Klipp is throwing a tantrum because she has failed to win at Hungry Hungry Hippos for the second time that morning. She is waving her skinny arms wildly and scolding her imaginary team for their failure to properly react to the attacking manoeuvres of the tiny balls.

'School boy defending!' she shrieks at the gormless plastic herbivores.

I place my arm gently on her father's forearm. 'Perhaps you should let her win the next one?'

He rears back abruptly in shock. I rarely see him angry and have forgotten what a magnificent sight it is. 'You are asking me to throw the match? This is an unbelievable question you have asked me.'

He slams his open palm down onto the table and then stands up and walks away.

He's right, of course, but I am stunned by the ferocity of his anger. Klipp copies his handslamming gesture and the hippos tremble on the table, their hinged mouths hanging open in shock.

Seconds later he is back in the room. 'I'm sorry,' he says simply. 'I do not mean to take it out on you but when I see her behave like that when she loses . . . I know it is not right.'

'She just needs to learn—' I begin, but he is barely hearing me and cuts me off.

'She does. It is part of my job to manage her reactions better.'

I smile, anticipating the printed-out training schedule that will no doubt appear on our fridge within hours. 'Yes, and then she will be able to lose with grace,' I say.

He looks at me, that eyebrow raised, 'No, if she had better reaction times then she wouldn't have to learn how to lose.'

I don't know how he's ever going to spend all of the respect he can't help but earn.

He settles Klipp onto his lap and resets the little plastic game, 'You see my darling,' he says to her gently, 'it's a game of two halves . . .'

Later that night I teach him how to not mind at all when balls fly into a mouth. Absolutely no one is losing now.

I'd be very interested in bettering myself if I was married to someone so sensible . . .

'I think I've spent too much time scrolling on Twitter today. I should get out and do something.'

'You are welcome to join me on my run if you like?'

And then, all of a sudden, there is nothing I want to do more than spend too much time scrolling through Twitter.

At Christmas he'd need absolutely no persuading to put on the red suit . . .

It's Christmas Eve. That most beautiful of nights, associated with peace and love throughout the land. However, we have a two-year-old and are staying with my parents.

Like most families on Christmas Eve we are playing our favourite game. The basic premise is that my mother has to criticise my parenting, but make the whole thing seem like it's a nonchalant conversation with my daughter. My role in the game is to be completely deaf. Mum wins if I even so much as raise an eyebrow, and she is the Queen of Christmas if I say any words in retaliation. Of course, the overall loser is my daughter, who will pay thousands of pounds to a therapist one day when I have told her all of the things I dislike about my mother and then continued to become an exact replica.

'Oh, she's not letting you have biscuits this close to bedtime is she?' sing-songs my mother in a falsetto tone at the perfectly happy toddler. It's hard to make out the sound of her favourite axe grinding over the sound of my teeth mashing against each other. 'Doesn't she know about how much sugar is in those things?' she coos relent-lessly at the oblivious child. 'How could she? She's too busy with her job to have time to make you homemade things, isn't she?'

My jaw tightens and I feel my spine ratcheting tighter and tighter. My chiropractor will never forgive me for undoing three long years of work with just two nights back at my childhood home.

There is a hand on my lower back, a gentle pres-sure reminding me that I am loved and supported and that there are options other than tearing every hair out of her head one by one. He swoops into the room and lifts Klipp to the ceiling where she giggles, spraying biscuit crumbs all over my moth-er's freshly swept floor. She wants to tut, I can feel

Laura Lexx

it brewing in her, but she cannot tut at my husband for he is not her blood.

He turns an icy stare on my mother. 'If you want to criticise my wife and her parenting then please do it directly and do not use our daughter as a pawn. Also, I really like how you have applied this make-up on your eyes with these flicks today. It enhances the blue in your irises to maximum effect.' He leaves the room, grabbing a biscuit for himself on the way out.

My mother is disarmed; dumbfounded by being confronted but thrown out of the rage by the compliment about her eyes. Perhaps I am not winning any awards for greatest mother, or daughter, but I am undoubtedly the greatest chooser of husbands on planet earth.

Our tradition is to each open one gift on Christmas Eve as a nod to my husband's German heritage. I detach my mother's non-recyclable paper from the gift she has handed me and look at the *Mrs Brown's Boys* DVD in my hand.

'Because you like comedy,' says my mother, and I have no idea if she doesn't know me at all or knows me so well she can use it to her advantage. 'I thought you might be able to get some tips from it.'

I am Schrödinger's Daughter: too successful to be a good mother, but nowhere near successful enough to be successful.

'My career is going well, Mum,' I say, gently but firmly. 'Just because I haven't been on *Mock the Week* it doesn't mean I've failed. In fact, I have several interviews for different writing positions and jobs coming up.'

Later on, as they make a cup of tea, my husband repeats literally the same words I have said, but to him she listens and does not bring it up for almost a day and a half.

Klipp is awake at 5 a.m. on Christmas Day, but I manage to sneak her downstairs and into the conservatory without so much as a floorboard creaking. I have the child-smuggling skills of a ninja border runner. I entertain her within the tiny room as the sun rises, using every skill I can muster to keep her quiet and occupied.

At 6.30 a.m. sharp I am joined by my co-parent. He sits with us on the floor with the building blocks and puts together an impressive multi-coloured approximation of Anfield.

At 9 a.m. my mother comes down the stairs, fully ready for the day. 'Merry Christmas,' she says brightly. 'Goodness me, not even dressed yet? Surely I raised you better than that.'

It takes every muscle in my husband's skilled fingers to bring my shoulders back down from my ears to their usual level.

'I'll get dressed in a moment,' I say to her, trying to keep my voice serene and even. 'I just wanted to keep Klipp quiet down here so she didn't disturb Dad.' I am careful not to insinuate that she has any part to play.

'Fat chance of that,' she says, switching on the oven. 'We've been awake since five when you two stomped down the stairs slamming every door as you went.'

Of course. I would like to sigh, but her bat ears would hear it as a hurricane. Instead I just scoop Klipp up and begin to head upstairs to get her dressed. My husband relieves her weight from my arms and props her on his hip instead.

'Let me get her dressed,' he says. 'You should go back to bed for a bit as you have let me have a lie-in.'

I smile at what a great team we are. We are a

top-flight couple. Not a chance of relegation here. My mother is quick to pounce.

'Oh, it's alright for you women with your modern husbands – you'd never have caught your father letting me have a lie-in.'

I open my mouth to retaliate, but his tongue is quicker off the mark than mine. 'If you were my wife I would let you sleep forever,' he says and then sweeps out of the room before she can work out what he means. I make a mental note to add a gift that can't be wrapped to his pile.

Later, we are sitting round the dinner table, paper hats in place and plates piled high. Klipp is wailing about two whole sprouts being near the food she actually intends to eat. I make a move to remove them from her plate; it would be nicer to listen to Mum's Alexander Armstrong CD than her screeches.

'Oh, your mum isn't giving in to you . . .' my mother begins immediately, picking up her double-act with Klipp. A single icy glance from my beloved stops her in her tracks. Her lip quivers. So do mine.

I remove the offending vegetables from Klipp's plate and set them to one side. 'Klipp,' I say, looking at my daughter sternly, 'you can either eat these with everything else or you can eat them afterwards but you are going to have to eat them.'

She eyes me cautiously, unsure of how seriously to take me. My please-don't-show-me-up-in-front-of-your-grandmother face seems to be working, because her little shoulders relax and she allows me to put one sprout back near the potatoes.

'Good girl,' I say. 'Just take it one ball at a time.'

'She's a credit to you,' says my mother, nodding at her plate. Unable to give me a compliment and look me in the eye simultaneously.

I catch my husband's eye and it's very clear I am his man of the match today and every day. I shiver as I think about the Christmas stockings I packed that weren't for Klipp. I have a feeling that later on a creature will be stirring much bigger than a mouse.

We volunteer to do the washing up while Klipp has a nap and Mum and Dad watch the Queen's speech. He washes while I dry, and his thorough approach to the application of the sponge causes the tea towel to tremble in my hands. One by one the plates disappear into the soapy water and reappear reprieved of their grimy burden. His hand

sweeps in ever-expanding circles around the porce-
lain surfaces, forging shining pathways through
the gravy slick. Nothing can slow him: neither red
cabbage stain nor cauliflower cheese globs. Nimble
fingers bury themselves in mugs, persevering with
the complicated tango between strong bone struc-
ture and delicate china. Sharp knives disappear
beneath the bubble spray and are met with extrav-
agantly fluent strokes down the entire length of
their smooth bodies; they reappear glinting –
dangerous but tamed. He needs no reminding to
wash the outsides of the saucepans. He is marvel-
lous to watch; John the Baptist in reindeer knit-
wear. He turns his eyes on me and I imagine him
plunging me into the frothing sink; scrubbing my
skin and focusing on the really, really grubby bits.

'You are off in a daydream, no?' he says to me
with a smile.

I vow that when I return home I will take a
sledgehammer to our dishwasher.

We spend the evening lazily on the sofa watching films for children, even though Klipp went to
bed at seven. My parents have incessant questions
about the plot despite it being solely about a group

of animals trying to gather enough food for the winter and honestly not a twist more.

'I don't know when these modern films got so complicated,' grumbles my father, and I feel my back tense in anticipation of –

'When Tony Blair got elected,' says my mother without hesitation. 'He absolutely decimated the education system.'

I open my mouth to contest the idea that the Labour party had any direct influence on creative decisions at Pixar, but suddenly there's hot breath on my ear and soothing words riding its thermals to conduct me towards my better judgement. 'Not every argument you could have is worth having,' he whispers. 'You cannot be every player on the pitch.'

My body relaxes back into the hard muscles of his. I smile up at Mum and nod noncommittally. 'The timing certainly is suspicious,' I say and she huffs contentedly and goes back to cheering for the ants' socialism despite always having cast her real political vote for the grasshoppers.

An hour later goodnight kisses are exchanged and Mum and Dad head up to bed.

'Shall we go to bed too?' asks my love. I have never said no to this question and follow him up the stairs to our bedroom with its matching guest towels and eighteenth-century mattress. As I brush my hair a vague feeling of insecurity washes over me.

'Do you think Klipp had a good day?' I ask him.

'She consumed 3,400 calories and received a literal sack of new toys,' he replies. 'Of course she had a good day. Why would you worry otherwise?'

'Do you ever think she's lonely?' My question is loaded, but he has a Premier League mind and catches my drift immediately.

I lean into my pillows and begin moisturising my hands in case moisturiser isn't the long con I think it might be. He climbs into the bed next to me, still full of thought from my proposition, and I patiently wait for his answer. He says nothing, but kisses me lightly on the mouth and it's clear that for tonight my transfer window is wide open.

Acknowledgements

I'm worried about writing this page because I don't want to seem too mushy, but let's face it: the only people reading this are people secretly hoping they'll be mentioned, so I suppose I can stop worrying. The funny thing to do would be to just write, 'Thanks to me for being brilliant and talented enough to write this book', but I'm fearful it wouldn't come across as tongue-in-cheek as I'd like.

As you can tell I worry a lot; from my career, to my weight, to the future of the planet, I worry on a nonstop loop. I hope this book will be a little light relief for other people who are also worriers. I can't stress enough how much this book isn't about wishing a man would ride in and fix all my problems: it's a little diary of all the ways my irrational brain tries to swipe at me and some of the ways I've learned to shut it up. You can always ask for help with your thoughts, and a good place to start is www.mind.org.uk

I'm very grateful to so many, many people, but mainly I am always grateful for Tom, my husband (in real life). He is my absolute constant source of confidence, love and entertainment. I'm very sorry my first book was about being married to someone else, my darling, but it would never have been written if you didn't love me. Everything is because you love me. Also, thanks for explaining all about football to me fifteen times a day while I wrote this – I promise to never ask you a question about the difference between a penalty and a free kick ever again.

Thank you to Diana for being an excellent team behind me, finding me this opportunity and talking me through every step of it. Thank you Andrew and Jo for your unending faith in my career – what an exciting new chapter we're in now (literally). Thank you to Kate and Lisa for welcoming me with so much glee to Two Roads. From that first (online) meeting I just fizzed with how cool it was that you would want to work with me. Kate, thank you for your patience and your notes and your gentleness with me. I'm not good with criticism and you've managed to shape this into a book without upsetting a stand-up comedian. That's impressive. I'm sorry for all the utter filth you've waded through.

And, Mr Klopp, I have no idea if you will ever

read this book, or know of its existence, but on the off-chance those are your eyes scanning this: thank you. You seem very cool. I like you. Not in a weird way, despite this book-shaped evidence to the contrary. Thank you for being a role model, for putting some sanity into the world, and for not getting in touch to ask me not to write this book. I wish you and your wife a lifetime of happiness and several more football trophies (cups?).

Thank you to everyone who has been so positive and made me believe this book could be a reality. 2020 certainly hasn't been what any of us expected, but thank you to everyone who made it so I could be that nobhead that actually did write a novel during lockdown.

About the Author

Laura Lexx is an award-winning comedian, actor and writer who lives in Brighton. She has a real husband who is real, brilliant, handsome and typing this.

Laura has had four critically acclaimed solo stand-up shows at the Edinburgh Fringe Festival. Her most recent two, *Trying* and *Knee Jerk*, both received multiple 5* reviews and won her Best Performer in the Comedian's Choice Awards two years in a row. She has also appeared widely on TV and radio, from *Live at the Apollo* and *Hypothetical* to *Roast Battle* and *The Comedy Club*.

Her debut novel, Pivot, will be published by Two Roads in 2022.